*Nita Mehta*
Cook with Confidence

# SINDHI
# K H A A N A

## VEGETARIAN

TEMPTING SINDHI RECIPES WITH
PHOTOS & DETAILED PREPARATION...

Recipes by: Neetu Mamtani

First Edition 2009

ISBN 978-81-7676-100-0 *Nita Mehta*
Cook with Confidence

*Food Styling and Photography:*

*Layout and Laser Typesetting:*

National Information
Technology Academy
3A/3, Asaf Ali Road
**N.I.T.A.** New Delhi-110002
☎ 23252948

*Published by:*

*Nita Mehta*
Cook with Confidence

3A/3 Asaf Ali Road, New Delhi-110002
Tel: 91-11-23250091, 29214011, 23252948, 29218574
Fax: 91-11-29225218, 91-11-23250091
E-Mail : nitamehta@email.com,   nitamehta@nitamehta.com
Website : http://www.nitamehta.com,   http://www.snabindia.com

*Contributing Writers :*
Anurag Mehta
Subhash Mehta

*Editorial & Proofreading :*
Rakesh
Ramesh

*Cover Designed:*
Rachna Panchal

*Distributed by :*

THE VARIETY BOOK DEPOT
A.V.G. Bhavan, M 3 Con Circus,
New Delhi - 110 001
Tel : 23417175, 23412567; Fax : 23415335
Email: varietybookdepot@rediffmail.com

*Printed by :*
MANIPAL PRESS LTD

Rs. 125/-

*Dedicated to my Father*
*Late Shri K. B. Juriasingani*

- Neetu Mamtani

# Introduction

Sindhis are fond of eating and make the best of hosts; their cuisine being a reflection of that. Sindhi cuisine mainly comprises of a lot of onions and they are properly sauted in both dry as well as gravy dishes which makes the food very tasty. Sindhis usually serve a variety of *pakoras* to their guests. *Pakoras* are also eaten as a side dish accompanied by *dal* and *chappati*. Sindhi *papads* are a must with every meal, even with breakfast. Roasted *papads* are also served even when water is offered to anyone. At a time, Sindhis either eat rice or *chappatis*.

Enjoy the varied dishes of this delectable cuisine.

# CONTENTS

## ABOUT THE RECIPE
### WHAT'S IN A CUP?

**INDIAN CUP**
1 teacup = 200 ml liquid

**AMERICAN CUP**
1 cup = 240 ml liquid (8 oz.)

The recipes in this book were tested with the Indian teacup which holds 200 ml liquid.

## BREAKFAST
# 6

## SIDE DISHES
# 27

# ACCOMPANIMENTS
## Achaar, Rice & Breads
# 44

# MAIN COURSE
# 51

# SWEETS
# 94

breakfast

# BESAN JO CHILLO

*Pancakes made with gramflour.*

*Makes 4-5 chillas*

1 cup gramflour (*besan*)
1 onion - finely chopped, 2 green chillies - finely chopped
½ tsp dry mint powder or 3 tbsp fresh mint leaves - chopped finely
1 tbsp dry fenugreek leaves (*kasoori methi*) - crushed
1 tsp red chilli powder, ¾ tsp salt, or to taste

1. Mix all the ingredients in a bowl. Add about 1 cup water to make a thick batter. Mix well and keep aside for 5-10 minutes.

2. Heat a non-stick *tawa*, grease with oil. Remove the hot *tawa* from fire and pour a ladle (*karchhi*) of batter and immediately spread on the *tawa* into a round shape. Return to fire.

3. Cook on medium flame from both sides till done, about 4-5 minutes. Serve with tomato chutney.

# DAL
# PAKWAAN

*Channa dal served with crispy maida pakwaan which are like crisp papads. Imli-pyaaz chutney is served as an accompaniment.*

## Makes 20-22 pakwaan

1 cup split gram lentils (*channa dal*) - soaked for 20 minutes

1 tsp salt or to taste, 1 tsp turmeric (*haldi*) powder

### FOR ONION-TAMARIND CHUTNEY

2 walnut size balls of tamarind - soak in 1 cup water for 15 minutes and strained to get ¾ cup tamarind pulp

1 onion - finely chopped, 1 tsp red chilli powder, ½ tsp salt

### FOR PAKWAAN

2 cups refined flour (*maida*)

1 tbsp oil, 1 tsp carom seeds (*ajwain*)

oil for deep frying, 1½ tsp salt

½-¾ cup water for kneading

1. Boil *dal* in pressure cooker with 1½ cups water, salt and turmeric to allow 1 whistle. Reduce heat and cook for 10 minutes on low flame. Keep aside.

2. Mix together — onion, red chilli powder, salt and tamarind and keep aside.

3. For the pakwaan, place flour, 1 tbsp oil, carom seeds and salt in a *parat*. Mix well. Make a smooth and stiff dough using enough water. Cover and keep aside for 10-15 minutes.

4. Divide the dough into walnut size balls, and roll it very thinly with a rolling pin to a 6" diameter size. Prick with a fork to avoid puffing.

5. Heat oil in *kadhai* and deep fry on low flame till they are crisp like papad for about 5 minutes on low flame.

6. Serve dal and tamarind chutney with pakwaan.

# CHHURI DAL JO PARANTHON

*Moong dal stuffed in a parantha.*

*Makes 6 paranthas*

STUFFING

1 cup *dhuli moong dal*

2 green chillies - finely chopped, 2 tbsp coriander - finely chopped

1 tsp red chilli powder, 1 tsp mango (*amchoor*) powder

1 tsp turmeric (*haldi*) powder, 1 tsp salt, 2 tbsp oil

DOUGH

1½ cups wheat flour (*atta*), ¾ cups water

1 tsp red chilli powder, 1 tsp salt

1. Wash *moong dal*. Cook in a deep pan with 1¾ cups water. Bring to a boil.

2. Add salt and turmeric powder. Cover with a lid and cook on low heat for 6-8 minutes till it gets cooked and no water remains. If any water remains after the *dal* is done, dry it on high flame.

3. Place the dry *dal* in a bowl and add green chillies, coriander leaves, red chilli powder, dried mango powder in it and mix well.

4. Place wheat flour in a bowl along with 1 tsp each of red chilli powder and salt. Rub well with palm. Add water to the dough gradually and knead well to a soft elastic dough.

5. Roll out a ball. Put some filling and cover the filling. Roll out stuffed *paranthas* with the *dal* filling.

6. Heat *tawa* and fry *parantha* applying oil on both sides till crisp.

7. Serve *paranthas* with curds and Sindhi papad.

# SANYUN ALU

*Lightly sweetened vermicelli (seviyan) with savoury potatoes.*

*Serves 4-5*

FOR SEVIYAN

2 cups thin roasted *seviyan*, 2 tbsp oil for roasting *seviyan*

½ cup sugar or to taste, 1 cup water

FOR ALOO

4 medium sized potatoes - peeled and cut into small pieces

½ tsp salt, 1 tsp turmeric powder (*haldi*), 1 tsp red chilli powder

1 tsp coriander powder (*dhania*), oil for deep frying

1. Heat 2 tbsp oil in a *handi* and fry seviyan for 4-5 minutes on medium flame.

2. Add enough water so that seviyan is covered properly with water. Add sugar and cook for 2-3 minutes till they are dry. Keep aside.

3. Heat oil in *kadhai* and deep fry potatoes for about 5-6 minutes on medium flame till tender and golden brown in colour.

4. Remove from oil and immediately sprinkle salt, turmeric, red chilli powder and coriander powder. Sanyun Alu is ready and eaten together.

# BHORI

*Serves 2-3*

2 Sindhi ufraati rotis (page 50)

¼ -½ cup sugar

¼-½ cup *desi ghee*

*Crushed roti mixed with ghee and sugar. Perfect for children.*

1. Fold the *rotis* into quarters and flatten the cooked *roti* with the *belan* on *the chakla* itself.

2. Then crumble *rotis* with hand. Put them in a serving bowl.

3. Heat ghee. Pour hot *desi ghee* and sugar in the bowl on the crumbled chappatis and mix well.

---

TIP:    Remember to crumble rotis when they are hot and freshly made. This dish is very good for infants and growing up children.

# CHAWAR JE ATTE JO DODO

*Rice flour pancakes.*

*Makes 6-7*

2 cups rice flour (*chawal ka atta*), 1¼ cups water, approx.
2 green chillies - chopped, 2 tomatoes - finely chopped
1 tbsp chopped green coriander
1 tsp red chilli powder, 1 tsp *garam masala*, 1½ tsp salt

1. Mix all the ingredients in a bowl. Add enough water to it to make a thick batter. Mix well.

2. Heat a non-stick *tawa*. Grease with 1 tsp oil. Remove *tawa* from fire. Spread a small ladle full of batter on it. Return to fire. Cook till edges turn golden. Turn side and cook on the other side till done. Serve with coriander chutney.

# KATH JO PARANTHON

*Peels of bitter gourd stuffed in parantha.*

*Makes 3-4 paranthas*

½ cup kath (*karelas*) - scrape out the outer skin with a peeler

1 cup wheat flour, 1 small onion - finely chopped

1 green chilli - finely chopped, 1 tsp grated ginger

½ tsp salt or to taste, 1 tsp *amchoor* powder, 1 tsp red chilli powder

1. Sprinkle ½ tsp salt on the *karela* peels and keep aside for 30 minutes. Wash *karela* peels in water and squeeze them well. Place *karela* peels, onion, green chilli, ginger, salt, *amchoor* and red chilli powder in a bowl and mix well.

2. Make a small *roti* and stuff 2-3 tbsp stuffing, pick sides to cover it from all sides and roll it with a rolling pin to a *parantha* size.

3. Heat *tawa* & cook the *parantha* on both the sides applying oil till crisp. Serve with fresh curds.

# MAKKI
## JO DODO

*Makki ki roti.*

**Makes 6 medium**

2 cups maize flour *(makki ka atta)*, 4 flakes spring garlic - finely chopped
2 green chillies - finely chopped, 3 tbsp chopped green coriander
1¼ tsp salt, 2 tbsp oil, ¾ cup water to knead dough

1. Place all the ingredients for *roti* in a *parat* and make a soft dough by adding water.

2. Take a poly-bag and cut from sides to make 2 equal pieces. Divide dough into small balls and place one ball of the dough on a piece of polybag and cover with the second half of the poly-bag. Roll lightly with a rolling pin to a small thick roti (3" diameter).

3. Heat a non-stick *tawa* and grease with 1 tsp oil. Put roti on the *tawa*. Reduce heat and spread the roti on the *tawa* with hands until it reaches a good size. Alternately roll out the dough fully between two sheets of polythene before putting on the *tawa*. Turn side and cook from the other side. Serve with curds.

22

# ATTE JO CHILLO

*Wheat flour pancakes.*

*Makes 4-5 small chillas*

1 cup wheat flour

1 onion - finely chopped, 2 green chillies - finely chopped

1 tbsp green coriander - finely chopped

1 tsp red chilli powder, 1 tsp salt, 1¼ cups water

1. Mix all the ingredients in a bowl and make a thick batter of a pouring consistency by adding enough water.

2. Heat a non-stick *tawa. Grease* with 1 tsp oil and remove *tawa* from fire. Take a ladle full of batter and spread evenly on the *tawa*. Return *tawa* to fire and cook for 4-5 minutes on both sides on medium flame. Remove from *tawa* and serve with green coriander chutney.

# JAWAAR
## JO DODO

*Jovar flour roti.*

**Makes 6-8**

2 cups jawaar flour

½ cup onions - chopped, ½ cup spring garlic - chopped

1 tbsp coriander leaves - chopped, 2 green chillies - chopped

1 tsp red chilli powder, salt to taste

1. Mix all the ingredients with jawaar flour and knead to a dough with enough water.

2. Grease a non-stick *tawa* with 1 tsp oil. Keep *tawa* on medium heat.

3. Take a big ball of the dough and make a *roti* between your palms and put it on the *tawa*. Dip your fingers in water and spread the *roti* evenly on *tawa*.

4. Cook on both sides and serve with *dahi*.

26

side dishes

# BHE
## JO KOFTO

*Flattened balls of lotus stem.*

**Serves 4**

250 gm lotus stem *(bhe)* - peel and cut each into 1" pieces
½ cup milk, 1 tsp red chilli powder, 1 tsp turmeric powder *(haldi)*
1 tsp dried mango *(amchoor)* powder, 1 tsp coriander powder *(dhania)*
½ tsp salt or to taste, 2 green chillies - chopped
2 tbsp gramflour *(besan)*

1. Put *bhe* in a pressure cooker. Add ½ cup milk. Add about 4 cups water to cover the *bhe*. Pressure cook for 30 minutes. Remove from fire and let the pressure drop.

2. Strain water and pat dry bhe on a clean kitchen towel. Mash the boiled *bhe* to a paste. Mix *bhe* and all other ingredients. Shape mixture into round tikkis.

3. Grease a non-stick pan with oil. Cook koftas from both sides. Serve hot with *dal* & *chappatis*.

# KATH JI BHAJI

*Peels of bitter gourd cooked to make a side dish.*

Serves 4-5

250 gm kath (*karela*) - scrape outer skin and cut into ¼" thick rounds
1 large onion - finely chopped, 1 large tomato - finely chopped
1 green chilli - finely chopped, 1 tsp salt, 1 tsp turmeric (*haldi*)
1 tsp red chilli powder, 1 tsp coriander powder (*dhania*)
1 tsp *garam masala*, 2 tsp *amchoor*, 4-5 tbsp oil to shallow fry

1. Sprinkle ½ tsp salt on *karela* slices and keep aside for ½ hour. Squeeze the kath well. Heat 4-5 tbsp oil in a *kadahi* & shallow fry kath till brown. Drain on kitchen paper & keep aside.

2. In a non stick pan, heat 1 tbsp oil, add onion saute for 4-5 minutes till they turn pink. Add tomato and green chilli and cook for 3-4 minutes. Add salt and all masalas.

3. Add kath. Mix for 5 minutes on low flame. Add *garam masala* and remove from fire. Serve.

# VAANGAN TARYAL

*Fried slices of brinjal.*

### Serves 2-3

1 large round brinjal (300 gm), *bharte waala baingan*

MIX TOGETHER

¼ tsp salt, 1 tsp coriander (*dhania*) powder, 1 tsp *garam masala*
1 tsp red chilli powder, 1 tsp amchoor powder, oil for deep frying

1. Cut the brinjal in ½ inch thick roundels. Make shallow diagonal cuts on each round in opposite directions to get diamond incisions, but do not cut too deep to separate. Sprinkle 1 tsp salt on them and keep aside.

2. Mix all the powdered masalas in a bowl and keep aside.

3. Heat oil in a *kadhai* and deep fry 2-3 brinjal slices at a time. Remove from oil on kitchen paper. Immediately sprinkle the powdered masala on the hot brinjal slices and serve.

# ALU TOK

*Fried crispy potatoes.*

*Serves 2-3*

250 gm small size potatoes - peel and cut each into 2 big pieces
1 tsp salt, oil for deep frying

MIX TOGETHER
1 tsp red chilli powder, 1 tsp coriander (*dhania*) powder
1 tsp dried mango (*amchoor*) powder

1. Prick potatoes with a fork and sprinkle 1 tsp salt. Mix and marinate them for half an hour.

2. Mix together all the masalas in a bowl.

3. Heat oil in a *kadhai*, fry 5-6 potato pieces in one batch till golden. Remove from oil and let them cool down.

4. Press each piece between the palms and refry on medium heat till brown and crisp. Take out the potatoes from oil and sprinkle the mixed masalas. Serve hot with *dal* and *chappatis*.

# SINDHI TIKKI

*Channa dal stuffed in alu tikki.*

*Makes 6-8 tikkis*

½ kg potatoes - boiled

3-4 bread slices

1 tsp salt

FILLING

4 tbsp bengal gram dal, ½ tsp salt

2-3 green chillies - chopped

1 tbsp green coriander - chopped

2 tsp mint leaves - chopped

1 tsp red chilli powder

1 tsp dried mango (*amchoor*) powder

1. Mash the boiled potatoes well till smooth.

2. Dip the bread slices in water for a second and squeeze out all the water. Add to the mashed potatoes. Add 1 tsp salt and mix well. Keep aside.

3. For the filling, wash *dal* well, place in a pressure cooker with ½ tsp salt and ½ cup water and give one whistle. Reduce flame and cook for another 10 minutes. Remove from fire and let the pressure drop by itself. Drain *dal* and place in a bowl.

4. Add coriander, mint leaves, green chillies and powdered masalas to the boiled *dal* and mix well.

5. Take a handful of mashed potatoes and flatten it with your palms. Put the stuffing of *dal* in it and close it properly from all sides, give it a shape of a round tikki.

6. Heat oil in a *kadhai* and deep fry the tikkis for 2-3 minutes on medium flame till golden brown. Remove from oil and serve hot.

---

TIP:    You can also put dal in a bowl and arrange it with potatoes and boil.

38

# ARBI
# TARYAL

*Fried arbi Sindhi style.*

*Serves 4*

500 gm colocassia *(arbi)*, 1 tsp salt
1 tsp red chilli powder, 1 tsp coriander powder *(dhania)*
1 tsp dried mango *(amchoor)* powder
oil for deep frying

1. Boil *arbi* in water for 10 minutes. Peel.

2. Sprinkle 1 tsp salt and let it marinate for 30 minutes at least.

3. Heat oil in a *kadhai* and half fry the *arbis*. Press each *arbi* between your palms. Now deep fry again till crisp.

4. Mix all the powdered masalas and sprinkle on each *arbi*.

39

# SANNA
# PAKORAS

*Pakoras fried in Sindhi style.*

*Serves 4*

1 potato - finely chopped, 1 onion - finely chopped, oil for frying

2 cups gramflour (*besan*), 1 tbsp chopped green coriander

2-3 green chillies - finely chopped

½ tsp dry mint leaves or 2 tbsp fresh mint leaves - chopped

1 tsp whole coriander seeds, 1 tsp black pepper corns

1 tsp *anardana* - roughly crushed, 1½ tsp salt, 1 tsp red chilli powder

1. Place all the ingredients in a bowl. Mix well. Add about ¾ cup water and make a thick batter.

2. Heat oil in a *kadhai*. Take a tablespoon full of batter and deep fry big (kebab size) pakoras in 2-3 batches on medium flame for 2-3 minutes till half done.

3. Remove from oil. Let them cool for 2-3 minutes. Break each pakora into 2-3 small pakoras and deep fry again in batches till golden, crisp and fully cooked. Serve hot with green chutney.

# VEGETABLE PAKORAS

*Makes 30-35*

1 stick of *bhe,* 1 medium sized potato, 1 medium sized *tinda*
1 medium sized onion, 1 small size long brinjal
8-10 florets of cauliflower, 2 tsp salt, 1 tsp red chilli powder
3-3½ cups gramflour (*besan*), 1½-2 cups water, oil for deep frying

1. Wash and peel *bhe* and potato. Cut them and *tinda*, onion, brinjal also into slices. Place all these vegetables and cauliflower in a bowl with ½ tsp salt and ½ tsp red chilli powder, mix and leave aside for 2-3 minutes.

2. Mix gramflour, 1½ tsp salt and ½ tsp red chilli powder in a bowl with about 1½ cups of water and make a thick *pakora* batter.

3. Heat oil in a *kadhai*. Dip each vegetable slice except cauliflower, into gramflour batter and fry for 3-4 minutes on medium flame till golden brown and crisp and fully cooked.

4. For cauliflower dip each floret into gramflour batter, deep fry lightly for 2-3 minutes till half done. Remove from oil, cool slightly and press each of them between your palms. Deep fry again for 2-3 minutes on medium flame till golden brown, crisp and fully cooked from inside. Serve with chutney.

# accompaniments
## achaar, rice & breads

# RAI PAANI
## JI ACHAAR

*Oil free onion pickle made of water and mustard seeds.*

*Makes 1 bottle*

20-25 small onions - peel and cut into halves or keep whole

½ cup mustard seeds (*rai*) - grind

2 tsp salt, 2 tsp turmeric (*haldi*) powder

2 tsp red chilli powder

1. Mix all the ingredients of *achaar* with onions. Put in a small dry, air tight glass container and add some water. Keep it in the sun for 2-3 days.

2. The oil free pickle is ready to be consumed within a week.

45

# TAHIRI

*Sweet rice prepared during pujas. Especially for Bhahraana Saheb Puja.*

*Serves 2-3*

1 cup rice - washed and soaked in 2 cups of water for at least 1 hour
1 cup crushed or grated gur
½ tsp salt, 1 tbsp oil

1. Heat 1 tbsp oil in a cooker.

2. Add ½ cup water and *gur* and stir till it dissolves. When the gur dissolves fully in water add rice along with the water in which it is soaked. Add salt and bring to a boil.

3. Cover and cook on low flame for 15 minutes till rice gets tender. Stir rice once in between.

# BHUGGAL CHAWAR

*Pulao with lots of sauted onion.*

*Serves 3-4*

1½ cups rice - soaked in water for 30 minutes

1 black cardamom (*moti illaichi*), 2 cloves (*laung*)

1 tsp cumin (*jeera*), 4 medium onions thinly sliced

2 tsp red chilli powder, 1½-2 tsp salt, 4 tbsp oil

1. Heat oil in a *sipri* (heavy bottomed *handi*). Add cardamom, cloves and cumin. Cook for a minute till they start spluttering. Add onions and saute for 5-7 minutes on medium flame till they turn darkish brown.

2. Add red chilli powder and 3 cups water. Bring to a boil.

3. Drain rice. Add rice and salt. Cover and cook for 12-15 minutes on low heat till the water is absorbed and the rice is done. Serve with chanyan ji dal.

# SINDHI UFRAATI ROTI

*Ghee stuffed roti. Perfect for carrying in a tiffin.*

*Makes 4 thick rotis*
1 cup wheat flour, 3 tbsp *ghee*

1. In a *paraat*, knead wheat flour with water slowly to make a soft dough.

2. Take a small ball of dough and roll it with a rolling pin and make a small *roti*.

3. Spread 1 tsp of *ghee*, pick sides and cover it properly and roll it again into a thick roti.

4. Place the *roti* on hot *tawa* and cook for 2 minutes, turn and cook for 2-3 minutes till brown patches appear. Remove from *tawa*.

5. Spread *ghee* on the *roti* before serving. Sindhi *rotis* are generally thick.

main
course

# TORI DAL
## BASSAR

*Ridge gourd with onion and onion and channa dal. Serve with plain rice.*

### Serves 4

250 gm *tori* - peeled & chopped, 1 cup *channa dal* - soaked for 20 minutes
1 tbsp oil, 2 onions - chopped finely, 2 tomatoes, 2 green chillies
salt to taste, 1 tsp red chilli powder, 1 tsp coriander (*dhania*) powder
1 tsp turmeric (*haldi*) powder

1. Grind tomatoes and green chillies together.

2. In a pressure cooker, heat 1 tbsp oil, saute onions till soft.

3. Add tomatoes and salt and cook for 5 minutes. Put all the masalas.

4. Drain *dal*. Add *dal* and saute for 5 minutes, add the *tori* and saute for 2-3 minutes. Add 1 cup water and pressure cook for 15 minutes. Mash the *tori* with a masher before serving.

# SEHAL
# BHE

*Subzi of lotus stem and potatoes with lots of onion and tomato.*

*Serves 4*

1 medium *bhe* - sliced, 2 medium sized potatoes - each cut into 4
4 onions - chopped, 2 tomatoes - grind to a paste
2 green chillies - chopped, salt to taste, 1 tsp *degi mirch*
1 tsp turmeric powder (*haldi*), 1 tsp coriander powder (*dhania*)
1 tsp *garam masala*, oil for cooking, 1 tbsp green coriander for garnishing

1. Heat 3 tbsp oil in a pressure cooker, add onions and saute till they turn soft.
2. Add tomatoes and salt to taste and stir for 5-6 minutes till oil separates.
3. Now add all the masalas and stir for a minute.
4. Add *bhe*, saute for 2 minutes.
5. Add potatoes and saute well till oil separates.
6. Add 2 cups water and pressure cook for 15 minutes. Garnish with coriander leaves.

53

# SAI
# BHAJI

*Green spinach with channa dal and assorted vegetables.*

*Serves 4-5*

1 bundle (650-700 gm) spinach - washed and chopped

1 cup *channa dal* - soaked for 10 minutes, salt to taste,

1 onion - chopped, 1 tomato - chopped, 2 green chillies - chopped

1 cup mixed vegetables (potato, cabbage, carrot) - chopped

TEMPERING

1 tsp red chilli powder, 4 garlic cloves - chopped

1. In a pressure cooker, put *channa dal*, onion, tomato, green chillies, vegetables and spinach. Add salt and 1 cup water. Pressure cook for 20 minutes. Remove from fire and let the pressure drop. Mash the spinach with masher. Keep aside.

2. In a pan heat 2 tbsp oil and put garlic, when it turns pink, put red chilli powder. Remove from fire and pour it into the spinach. Serve hot with plain rice and roasted papads.

# THOOM WARI BHINDI

*Garlic stuffed in lady fingers.*

*Serves 4-5*

250 gm lady fingers *(bhindi)*, 2 tbsp oil, 8-10 garlic cloves
2 green chillies, 1 tsp turmeric powder, 1 tsp dried mango powder
1 tsp red chilli powder, 1 tsp coriander powder, ½ tsp salt

1. Wash and cut the head and tail of the *bhindi's* and make a slit in the center.

2. In a *hamam-dasta* crush garlic and green chillies, add all the powdered masalas in it and salt.

3. Fill each *bhindi* with this stuffing.

4. In a pan, heat 2 tbsp oil, put the *bhindi's*, mix well and cook covered on low heat till tender.

# BHE ALU
# RAS PAYA

*Lotus stem and potatoes in gravy.*

*Serve 3-4*

250 gm *bhe* - peeled and cut diagonally into ¼" thick slices

2 potatoes - cut each into 4 pieces

2 onions - finely chopped

2 large tomatoes - finely chopped

2 green chillies - finely chopped

2 tbsp finely chopped green coriander

1 tsp red chilli powder

1-1½ tsp salt

2 tbsp oil

1. Boil *bhe* with 2 cups water, 1 tsp salt and 1 tbsp lemon juice in a pan for 10 minutes on medium flame.

2. Grind tomatoes and green chillies together in a mixer and keep aside.

3. In a pressure cooker, heat 2 tbsp oil. Add onions and saute for 5-10 minutes till they turn pink.

4. Add tomato-chilli paste and cook for 5 minutes on medium flame. Add salt, red chilli powder and mix well. Put boiled *bhe* and potatoes in it and saute for 3-4 minutes on high flame, stirring continuously.

5. Add 1½ cups water to keep the gravy thick and pressure cook for 20 minutes. Remove from fire. Garnish with coriander leaves and serve hot with rice.

# TINDA
# AUR JI RAI

*Tinda cooked with rai and garlic in gravy.*

*Serves 3-4*

250 gm *tinda* - peel and cut into 4 pieces

2 potatoes - peel and cut each into 4 pieces

5-6 garlic flakes - chopped

2-3 green chillies - chopped

5-6 tomatoes - roughly chopped

1½ tsp salt, 1 tsp red chilli powder, 1 tsp coriander powder

2 tbsp oil

1 tsp mustard seeds (*rai*)

1 tbsp finely chopped green coriander

1. Grind tomatoes, garlic and green chillies together in a mixer and keep aside.

2. In a pressure cooker heat 2 tbsp oil, add *rai*, when they start spluttering add tomato paste and salt. Saute for 5-6 minutes on medium flame till semi dry.

3. Add red chilli powder and coriander powder, saute for 2-3 minutes on medium flame till oil leaves the sides.

4. Now add coriander, *tinda* and potatoes. Stir for 2-3 minutes. Add 1½ cups of water to get a thick gravy. Pressure cook for 10 minutes on medium flame. Serve hot.

# BESAN JI
# TIKKI JI
# BHAJI

*Tikki made of gramflour and made into a subzi by putting it in a curry.*

*Serves 3-4*

TIKKIS

1 potato - very finely chopped

1 onion - very finely chopped, ½ cup gramflour (*besan*)

1 tsp pomegranate seeds (*anardana*) powder

1 tsp poppy seeds (*khus-khus*), 1 tsp salt, 1 green chilli - finely chopped

1 tbsp oil

GRAVY

4 onions - finely chopped

3 tomatoes - finely chopped

2 green chillies - finely chopped, 1 tbsp oil, 1 tsp red chilli powder

1 tsp coriander (*dhania*) powder, 1 tsp *garam masala*, 1½ tsp salt

1. Mix all the ingredients of tikki in a bowl. Mix well and make a thick paste. Add a few tbsp of water if needed.

2. Apply some oil on the palms and make 1½" small round tikkis and deep fry for 3-4 minutes till golden brown in colour. Keep aside.

3. For Gravy : Heat 1 tbsp oil in a *kadhai* and saute onions for 3-4 minutes till light golden.

4. Add tomatoes and cook for 5-7 minutes on medium flame till oil separates.

5. Add salt, red chilli powder, coriander powder and mix well.

6. Add the prepared tikkis.

7. Add 1½ cups water and bring to a boil, cover with a lid. Cook on slow flame for 10 minutes and serve hot.

# SINDHI
# CURRY

*Curry made with gramflour and tamarind with lots of vegetables.*

*Serves 6-7*

2 medium sized potatoes - each peeled and cut into 4

2 *tinda* - each peeled and cut into 4 pieces

2 *arbi* - peeled and each cut into 4 pieces

7-8 *bhindi* - cut and slit, 4-5 slices of *bhe*

4-5 french beans - cut into 1" pieces, 4-5 guvar - cut into 1" pieces

4-5 slices of brinjal, 2-3 green chillies

2 lemon size balls of tamarind - soak in ½ cup warm water for ½ hour

4-4½ cups of warm water, 3-3½ tbsp gramflour (*besan*)

1 tsp red chilli powder, 1 tsp turmeric powder (*haldi*)

1 tsp fenugreek seeds (*methi dana*), 1 tsp cumin (*jeera*)

a sprig of curry leaves, oil for deep frying, 4 tbsp oil, 1½ tsp salt

1. Heat oil in a *kadhai* and deep fry *arbi*, *bhindi* and brinjal separately for 4-5 minutes on medium flame. Keep aside.

2. Heat 4 tbsp oil in a pressure cooker, add fenugreek seeds and cumin. When they start spluttering add gramflour and roast on slow flame till golden brown.

3. Add 3 cups of water and keep stirring so that no lumps are formed. Add salt, turmeric, red chilli powder, curry patta, potato, *bhe* and *tinda*. Pressure cook to allow 1 whistle, reduce heat and cook for 5-7 minutes. Remove from fire and let the pressure drop by itself.

4. Mash the soaked tamarind and strain to get pulp. Add tamarind pulp to the curry and bring to a boil.

5. Add beans, guvar and whole green chillies. Simmer for 5-7 minutes. Add the fried vegetables. Serve with rice.

# CHANYAN
## JI DAL

*Channa dal cooked the Sindhi style.*

*Serves 4*

2 onions - finely chopped, 3 tomatoes - grind to a paste
1 green chilli - chopped, 1 cup *channa dal* - soaked for 15 minutes
1½ tsp salt, or to taste, 1 tsp turmeric powder (*haldi*)
1 tsp degi mirch, 1 tsp coriander powder (*dhania*)
1 tbsp oil for cooking, 1 tbsp coriander leaves for garnishing

1. In a pressure cooker heat 1 tbsp oil and saute onions for 4-5 minutes till soft and transparent.

2. Add tomatoes and green chilli and saute for 2-3 minutes.

3. Add salt, turmeric powder, degi mirch and coriander powder. Add dal and saute for 2 minutes.

4. Add 2½ cups water and pressure cook for 15 minutes. Remove from fire. Garnish with coriander leaves and serve.

# BHINDI
## SEHAL

*Subzi of lady finger with potatoes in lots of onion and tomato.*

*Serves 4*

20 *bhindi* - cut head and make a slit for stuffing

4 potatoes - peeled and cut into slices

4 onions - finely chopped

3 tomatoes - grind to a paste

oil for deep frying

1¾ tsp salt, or to taste, 1 tsp turmeric (*haldi*) powder

1 tsp coriander (*dhania*) powder, 1 tsp degi mirch

1 tsp *garam masala,* 1 tbsp green coriander for garnishing

STUFFING

1 tsp turmeric (*haldi*) powder, 1 tsp amchoor powder

1 tsp red chilli powder, 1 tsp coriander (*dhania*) powder

1. Deep fry *bhindi* and potatoes in separate batches till cooked properly. Fry each batch for 3-4 minutes and keep aside.

2. Mix masalas for stuffing and fill into the *bhindi's*.

3. In a *kadhai* heat 1 tbsp oil and saute onions till soft.

4. Add tomatoes and salt and stir for 5-7 minutes till oil separates.

5. Put rest of the masalas - salt, turmeric powder, coriander powder, degi mirch and *garam masala*.

6. Add *bhindi* and potatoes, mix well. Cover and cook on low heat for 2-3 minutes till both the vegetables blend properly. Garnish with coriander and serve.

# TRI DAL

*Three dals mixed together.*

*Serves 3-4*

½ cup *channa dal*

¼ cup *kali urad chilka dal*

½ cup *katti moong chilka dal*

5-6 cloves garlic - finely chopped

1 onion - finely chopped

1 green chilli - finely chopped

1 tsp degi mirch powder

1 tsp turmeric (*haldi*) powder

1½ salt

1 tbsp *desi ghee*

1. Wash and soak all dals together in a bowl in 4 cups of water for 30 minutes.

2. Pressure cook dal along with soaked water, salt and turmeric to allow 1 whistle. Reduce heat and cook further on slow fire for 5-7 minutes. Remove from fire and let the pressure drop by itself.

3. Heat *desi ghee* in a pan, add onions and cook for 4-5 minutes till golden brown.

4. Add garlic and green chilli and stir, put degi mirch and mix well and pour over the *dal*. Serve hot with steamed rice.

# AANI JI
# BHAJI

*Diamonds made of besan*
*and dropped in gravy.*

*Serves 5-6*

FOR AANI

1 cup gramflour (*besan*)

a pinch of asafoetida (*hing*), 1 tsp carom seeds (*ajwain*)

1 tsp turmeric powder (*haldi*)

1 tsp pomegranate seeds powder (*anardana*), 1 tsp red chilli powder

½ tsp salt, 4 tbsp water to make the dough, oil for deep frying

FOR BHAJI

2 onions - finely chopped, 3-4 tomatoes - grind to a paste

1 green chilli - finely chopped, 1½ tsp salt

1 tsp coriander (*dhania*) powder, 1 tsp turmeric powder (*haldi*)

1 tsp degi mirch powder, 1 tsp *garam masala*

1 tbsp finely chopped green coriander

1. Mix all the ingredients for aani in a bowl and add water, little at a time to make a stiff dough.

2. Roll out dough into a big chappati between two sheets of polythene. Cut it into diamond shaped pieces.

3. Heat oil in a *kadhai* and deep fry for 3-4 minutes on low flame in 3-4 batches. Keep aside.

4. Heat 2 tbsp oil in a *kadhai* and cook onions for 3-4 minutes till golden brown, add tomatoes and green chillies. Stir till oil separates.

5. Add salt and all the masalas and mix well for a minute. Add about 1½ cups water to get a thin curry. Bring to a boil. Keep curry aside till serving time.

6. To serve, boil the curry. Arrange the aanis on it and cover & cook on low heat for 6-8 minutes.

7. Garnish with chopped coriander and serve hot.

# SAI DAL

*Split green moong dal.*

*Serves 5-6*

1 cup green moong chilka - soaked for 10 minutes
3-3½ cups water, 1 tsp salt, 1 tsp red chilli powder
1½ tsp *amchoor* powder, 1 tsp coriander (*dhania*) powder

TEMPERING
1 tbsp *ghee*, 1 tsp cumin (*jeera*)

1. Place the dal, salt and water in a pressure cooker and give 2 whistles. Reduce heat and cook for another 5 minutes on low flame. Remove from fire and let the pressure drop by itself.

2. In a serving bowl, pour cooked *dal*. Mix all masalas together and sprinkle on dal.

3. Heat *ghee* in a pan and add cumin. When it splutters pour it on the *dal* and serve hot.

# KARELA
## SEHAL

*Subzi of bitter gourd and potato with lots of onion and tomato.*

*Serves 4-5*

250 gm bitter gourd (*karela*) - scrape outer skin lightly and cut into round slices, sprinkle 1 tsp salt and leave for one hour

2 potatoes - cut into round slices

3 medium sized onion - finely chopped

8-10 flakes of garlic - chopped

3 tomatoes - roughly chopped

2 green chillies - chopped

1 tsp salt, 1 tsp turmeric powder (*haldi*), 1 tsp red chilli powder

1 tsp *garam masala*

1 tbsp green coriander - finely chopped

2 tbsp oil

1. Grind tomatoes, green chillies and garlic together in a mixer. Keep aside.

2. Heat 2 tbsp oil and cook onions for 5-7 minutes on high flame till pink. Add *karela* and potato slices. Mix well.

3. Cover and cook on low flame for 10-15 minutes until both vegetables get tender. Add a sprinkling of water in between if needed.

4. Add tomato paste and cook for 5-7 minutes on high flame.

5. Add all the powdered masalas and mix well. Cook for a minute. Remove from fire.

6. Garnish with chopped green coriander and serve hot.

# KARELA RAS PAYA

*Bitter gourd in tomato and black pepper gravy.*

*Serves 4*

250 gm *karela*, 1 tsp mustard seeds (*rai*), 1 tbsp gramflour (*besan*)
4-5 tomatoes - grind to a paste, salt to taste, 1 tsp red chilli powder
1 tsp turmeric powder (*haldi*), 1 tsp coriander powder (*dhania*)
¼ tsp freshly crushed pepper, 1 tbsp coriander for garnishing

1. Peel the *karelas*. Cut into slices. Sprinkle salt & keep aside for 1 hour. Wash and squeeze well.

2. In a *kadhai*, heat 2 tbsp oil, add mustard seeds wait for a few seconds to stop spluttering. Add gramflour and saute till light golden. Add tomatoes and salt to taste and saute for 4-5 minutes.

3. Add turmeric, coriander, red chilli and black pepper and mix well. Add 2 cups water, bring to a boil, put *karelas*, simmer, and cover for 5 minutes. Garnish with green coriander and serve.

# KARELA CHANYAN JI DAL

*Serves 4*

1 cup *channa dal* - soaked for 20 minutes

3 small karelas - peeled and cut into halves lengthwise

½ cup wheat flour (*atta*), salt to taste, 1 tsp turmeric (*haldi*) powder

1 tsp *garam masala*, oil for deep frying,

1. Marinate *karela* with wheat flour for ½ hour. This helps to reduce bitterness.

2. Squeeze the *karelas*. Deep fry karelas and keep it aside.

3. Drain dal. Boil the dal with 2 cups water in a pressure cooker for 10 minutes to get a thick dal.

4. When dal is cooked, put the fried *karelas* and garam masala and cook for 5 minutes. Serve.

# VAANGAN
# PATATA

*Subzi of brinjal and potatoes.*

*Serves 3-4*

1 medium round brinjal - cut into 1-2 inch pieces

2 medium sized potatoes - cut into 1 inch pieces

3 medium sized tomatoes - grind to a paste

2 green chillies - chopped

1 tsp cumin (*jeera*)

1 tsp turmeric (*haldi*) powder

1 tsp degi mirch powder

1 tsp coriander (*dhania*) powder

1¼ tsp salt, oil for deep frying

1 tsp finely chopped green coriander

1. Marinate potatoes and brinjal with 1 tsp salt for 10 minutes. Remove and squeeze out all salt.

2. Heat oil in a *kadhai* and deep fry both potatoes and brinjal separately for 3-4 minutes on medium flame and keep it aside.

3. Heat 2 tbsp oil in a pan add cumin, when it splutters add tomatoes, salt and cook for 8-10 minutes on medium flame till oil separates.

4. Add degi mirch, turmeric powder, coriander powder, ¼ tsp salt and cook for a minutes.

5. Now add brinjal and potatoes and mix well for 2-3 minutes on medium flame.

6. Garnish with coriander and serve hot with chappatis.

# GOBHI
# SEHAL

*Subzi of cauliflower and potatoes with lots of onion and tomato.*

*Serves 3-4*

1 medium sized cauliflower (500 gm) - cut into medium florets

2 medium sized potatoes - cut into ½" cubes

3 medium sized onion - finely chopped

3 medium sized tomatoes - grind to a paste

2 green chillies - cut into thin long slices

½ cup water, 1 tbsp ginger-garlic paste

1 tsp turmeric powder (*haldi*), 1 tsp red chilli powder

1 tsp coriander powder (*dhania*), 1½ salt,

1 tsp *garam masala*, 2 tbsp oil

1 tbsp finely chopped green coriander

1. Heat 2 tbsp oil in a *kadhai* and add onions cook for 5-7 minutes till light golden.

2. Add ginger-garlic paste and cook for 3-4 minutes on medium flame.

3. Add the potatoes, salt & turmeric powder, cover and simmer for 5 minutes on medium flame.

4. Now add cauliflower. Stir to mix well. Add ¼ cup of water and mix well and cover for 15 minutes on medium flame till potatoes and cauliflower are tender.

5. Add all the powdered masalas, mix well and cook for a minute.

6. Now add the ground tomatoes and sliced green chillies and cook for 5-6 minutes on high flame till water is absorbed.

7. Take out in a serving dish and garnish with coriander leaves. Serve hot.

sweets

# SINDHI LADOO

*Ladoos made with wheat flour.*

*Makes 20-25 ladoos*

3 cups wheat flour (*atta*)
1 cup melted *ghee*
1 cup sugar
½ cup chopped nuts (*kaju*, *badam* and pista)

1. Roast wheat flour along with *ghee* in a *kadhai* till golden brown for 10-12 minutes on medium flame. Remove from fire and spread in a tray to cool.

2. Grind sugar for just a few seconds to get a coarsely powdered sugar.

3. Add powdered sugar and nuts to the ladoo mixture. Mix well and take a handful of this mixture and make ladoos with it.

95

# SINGGAR JI MITHAI

*Burfi made with plain sev.*

*Serves 8*

½ kg singgar (thin plain sev, unsalted)
2 tbsp *ghee*
½ kg *khoya,* 3 cups sugar
4 cups water

1. Heat *ghee* in a big flat *kadhai*. Add singgar and stir continuously till it gets light brown and well roasted. Let it cool.

2. In a broad *kadhai*, heat water and sugar to make a sugar syrup to one thread consistency.

3. Put singgar in it. Mix well. Add *khoya* and mix well again.

4. Set this mixture in a *thali* and cut into square pieces.

# SATPURA

*Layered sweet.*

*Makes 5-6*

1 cup plain flour (*maida*)

¼ cup water, 1 tbsp oil

1 tbsp sugar

oil for deep frying

1. Place plain flour in a *paraat*. Add oil and rub it properly. Knead it with water by adding little at a time to make a soft dough.

2. Take a little ball from the dough and roll it with a rolling pin to make a small roti. Cut roti into seven ½ inch broad strips. Place all the strips on one another and roll it again into a poori size.

3. Heat oil and deep fry satpura for 3-4 minutes on medium heat. Take it out from oil and sprinkle sugar on it. Do this with rest of the dough and make satpuras.

# KHAKAR

*Sweet made of thin rotis.*

*Makes 8-10*

1 cup wheat flour
1/3 cup sugar
2 tbsp oil
oil for deep frying

1. Heat sugar with ¼ cup of water in a pan and stir till sugar dissolves in water. Remove from heat and keep aside to cool.

2. Take wheat flour, add oil and rub properly. Add the prepared sugar syrup little at a time and knead well to get a firm dough.

3. Take a small portion of the dough and roll it to get a thin roti.

4. Heat oil in a *kadhai* and deep fry 4-5 khakar for 3-4 minutes on medium flame till golden brown and crisp.

100

# CHHOTHE

*Sweet made with wheat flour and cut into quarters.*

*Serves 20*

2 cups wheat flour, ¼ cup plain flour (*maida*)

½ cup oil

2 tbsp chopped pista

8 tbsp sugar boiled with ¼ cup water

oil for deep frying

1. Boil water and sugar. Cook till sugar dissolves. Keep this syrup aside to knead the dough.

2. Mix together wheat flour, maida and oil. Add pista.

3. Gradually add the sugar syrup and knead well to a stiff dough.

4. Take a small portion of the dough and roll into a roti. Cut roti into quarters.

5. Deep fry on low heat till golden and properly cooked. Sprinkle sugar and chopped pistas on them to serve.

# GLOSSARY

| SINDHI NAMES | ENGLISH NAMES | SINDHI NAMES | ENGLISH NAMES |
|---|---|---|---|
| Atte | Wheat Flour | Sai | Green |
| Bassar | Onion | Sajji | Whole |
| Bhe | Lotus Stem | Sanna | Thin |
| Bhuggal | Saute | Singgar | Thin plain sev (besan) without salt |
| Chanyan ji Dal | Gram Lentils | | |
| Chawar | Rice | Sipri | Deep pan |
| Dodo | Round Roti | Taryal | Fried |
| Kath | Peels of Bitter Gourd | Thoom | Garlic |
| Sai Bhaji | Spinach | Tori | Ridge Gourd |
| | | Vaangan | Brinjal |